THE SUPERNOVA ADVANTAGE

THE SUPERNOVA ADVANTAGE

JIM STEPHENS

CONTENTS

CHAPTER 1

Introduction

First item of discussion will focus on the journey of the retail financial advisory practice, followed by a summary of the key objectives of the essay. Based on the experience gained from working with thousands of practices in some 47 countries, I can also state that practitioners who embrace the Supernova Approach to building a transformed operational structure for a more efficient practice, and who also embrace the Supernova Community model to grow their practices profitably, will increase their gross revenues by at least 40%. There will be a reduction in the number of hours or days they work, an increase in the proportion of recurring revenues to 60+% of their total revenues (for Protecting, Organising, and Growing), an increase in take-home personal income, and a drastic reduction in the time taken, on average, to deliver their solutions to clients.

The Journey of the Retail Financial Advisory Practice We should not take for granted that everyone reading this essay has similar life experiences. Indeed, very few people have started as a junior or a para-planner if employed in an existing practice; most left where they worked because they did not like something with the "way things are done around here." If you are contemplating entering a business partnership (or even just as an employee), it is not a bad idea to get to know and understand the values of the person you might be joining. In some ways, this essay can be termed as possessing many thought-leading ideas about where we have been and what may come next. If we can understand fully the past, then perhaps the future they face will be one of their own making, and thus, perhaps their very best future.

Understanding the Supernova Advantage

Do you wish to revamp your financial advisory practice? If so, the Supernova approach might be just what you're looking for. Supernova is a consultancy company that focuses exclusively on financial consultants and those who advise them on how to run their firms more effectively. The secret to their advice is centered on client improvement, revisions to support, assurance of compliance, and the implementation of technology. These elements make up what is also known colloquially as "The Supernova Advantage".

What are these components, you may wonder? Well, let us take a closer look at these four elements. As Supernova puts it, client mastery necessitates a widespread knowledge of customers' financial needs and perspectives. Support mastery is all about business solutions. This part of the Supernova Advantage involves a systemic revision of an advisor's support networks to ensure optimal service. This control and compliance focus centers on tech security, physical security, the technology of security, and privacy. Finally, the technology piece! Supernova has come out firmly in favor of custom settlements rather than off-the-rack solutions. So the learning charge for the financial planner is steep—but the results of implementing this advice appear to make it worthwhile.

He was willing to place his financial planning business under the microscope and testify that some of the guidance he's received from the Supernova organization is field tested, proving to have significantly improved efficiency, increased client relationships, and increased business. The Supernova technique is strongly based on customer acquisition, growth, and retention. This technique is not for everyone. It's not for you if you're not running a financial planning firm yet. It is not for you if you do not yet have a vivid image of what the average amount of commission or charges directly or indirectly attributable to the service should be.

CHAPTER 2

Foundations of a Successful Financial Advisory Pra

Advisors who build a thriving practice focused on financial success and happiness for themselves and their clients have unlocked 'The Supernova Advantage' and taken their practice to supernova levels. The Supernova Model is built on the bedrock of a strong foundation, Planet Building. To help you onboard new clients, your marketing is aligned with your principles, strategies, and tactics.

The key to any marketing is a set of principles and a plan. A Lightning Rod keeps your energy up and helps guard against burnout. First, let's start with the plan. What are the principles behind the Supernova Model's Planet Building? Digital Presence means if you're not online, you might not exist. We also transform your website into the heart of your marketing. Finally, staying connected in the digital age requires an intense and purposeful plan. Each of these principles has strategies and tactics to live it out. Every strategy is a communication tool that couches speaking potential customers' language and stirring up interest.

We suggest each of these SpeakEase tools has an event at its heart: "Stress Test March Madness," "Business Owner's Playbook," "Weekly Financial Boot Camp," and "Blueprint for Financial Success". See the Insets above for further detail on each event to keep your focus and energy on track. Once you have updated your plan based on your feedback and coaching, you need to stick with it and reboot a tortoise-like persistency resistance to impatience and fickleness.

Defining Your Value Proposition

Keep your clients strongly connected to your business and services. Adopt a client-centric approach where you can incorporate methodologies that maximize the value for your clients. To do so, keep up with their initiatives and what they want, and accordingly work to best service them so that your financial practice becomes a client-centred financial advisory practice. Another important strategy that can define your services and create value for clients is to plot your own unique pathway in the financial services industry. This is known as defining your value proposition, and it leads to understanding the perfect client, which is critical for the success of your financial advisory practice.

If you are hoping to attract relatively wealthy clients, small business owners, corporation executives, etc. to your financial advisor services, begin by performing the following primary steps of creating a narrative that explains these statements: - What are the financial concerns and opportunities your clients have to address? - What are the many aspects of their lives that your customized financial strategies will positively impact? - What strengths and opportunities do you bring to your practice that allow you to deliver the right financial solutions to your prospective clients? - What types of relationships do you most enjoy having with your clients? For you, the deliverer of financial advisory services, how do "crème de la crème" clients become "prospective clients" to be approached? In short, as we define a client-centric financial advisory practice, we will show you the "perfect clients" — the 'B's and 'C's — to whom you would like to deliver financial advisory services.

CHAPTER 3

Leveraging Technology for Efficiency

It's impossible to talk about the Supernova advantage without highlighting the powerful technology that enables financial advisors' practices to run so efficiently. While there are many great technology solutions useful for advisors, this competitive edge comes as a result of leveraging multiple, integrated tools and platforms. From NaviPlan to Applied Finance Group to Riskalyze—the components of the Supernova system are thoughtfully linked to simplify otherwise complex and time-intensive practices. It's able to drive new connections with our clients that we haven't had before," said Michael, a Supernova advisor, further validating the importance of technology in aiding us to bridge that gap between e-advice and field advice. By demonstrating the value of leveraging technology in a big way, it further aids us in making the point that our mission is to provide not just life insurance advice, or investments advice, or any other part of the e-advice spectrum, but broader financial advice.

In bringing additional value to advisors and the clients they serve, we will continue to leverage technology via our advice300 platform, which is a vehicle for our other operating platform, developed explicitly for this field advice community and combining the use of technology in support of our end goal of "good advice for all." Their enthusiasm for the benefits of efficiency coupled with the satisfaction intrinsically linked to a happy client base is unmistakable. As Dave, a fellow Supernova advisor mentioned, "It is fun to do the things we love doing." We have talked to many of our Fantex Supernova members and these words ring familiar time and again when asked about the Supernova advantage. The advisors who choose to partner with us recognize the forward-thinking approach Seattle offers the opportunity to adopt and understand that we are not afraid to capture the best talent, skills and connections from our market to work alongside our professional staff.

Key Technologies for Financial Advisors
The digital age has brought with it several essential technologies that have reformed business. These developments have considerably changed how professionals interact with their clients. Today, as mentioned so far, advisors can use SMS or messaging platforms to check in with clients in a way that is health-giving. Other entrepreneurs use SaaS tools to run their businesses from the Caribbean, taking contracts and building client relationships in clear living color via Zoom from afar. If you are not already using Zoom in your practice, consider including it going forward. Here's why: Zoom permits a financial advisor to videoconference in high-definition, allowing you to employ visual capabilities to position yourself as an educational authority.

While communicating with video, share your computer screen with clients to demonstrate the details of your financial plans, presentations, insurance solutions, and important illustrations, as illustrated at the Supernova. With only a few keystrokes, a mouse click or two, and your usual command of financial topics, you can also record the entire call and later post it to your website with a podcasting service so that it is available as content to help your website's visibility on search engines, independently drive traffic to your site via the tags and promotion in services like iTunes, and assist in branding your site. After recording the conversation as an MP3, you will also find it a cinch to transcribe the info on Rev.com or another similar site. You now have content that you can use in podcasts and on your blog. Your clients also have the ability to visit your online office and later share the information—myriad illustrations and more—with others, thereby referring new-focused clients to your site.

CHAPTER 4

Building and Maintaining Client Relationships

In any professional atmosphere, organizations are typically concerned with the most effective and efficient way to put their product and services in front of their potential clients and customers in a way that entices them not only to listen but to move forward with a purchase or commitment. Top financial professionals from around the United States are also concerned with the most effective and efficient way to approach potential clients and maintain the clients that they already have. Their industry has unique challenges and critical success factors when it comes to building and maintaining relationships with clients.

Developing rapport with clients & prospects A critical part of building confidence and trust in working with an advisor is camaraderie or "clicking" with the potential client. It is just after this first step of credibility and rapport has been established that a potential client or prospect is interested in learning about the product and services being offered. It makes sense that we can become comfortable with someone much easier if we share some commonalities based on familiar likes and desires - in fact, our "circle of comfort" is often drawn around people who are similar to us in age, appearance, clothing style, hobbies, and even political opinions. Our natural tendencies are to avoid people who are different in privacy and public spaces. The human mind must be comfortable with someone before we will listen to the problems they have solved for themselves - it is only after developing a sense that another has lived and experienced some of what we have that his opinions will be trusted. An individual will value the advice from another's experience above pure fact, and the aspect of sharing commonalities becomes more important the more personalized the service.

Effective Communication Strategies

Effective communication isn't just about talking – it's about being able to listen actively, empathize, and effectively communicate. Here are some tips on how to take your communication strategies to the next level.

Engage in active listening. Communicate that you are engaged by nodding your head. Be sure to maintain eye contact – it communicates trust and respect to the speaker. Empathize with the speaker by avoiding judgment, asking questions, and acknowledging the speaker's feelings. Feedback effectively by summarizing the speaker's comments. Ask follow-up questions, and openly share your thoughts on the conversation. Be supportive. It's not just important to hear your clients, but also to reassure them that they are being heard. Thank the client for sharing and sharing a solution, telling them, "While I may not have every answer you need right now, this is what I suggest." Vary your communication strategies. People have different learning and interpretation styles, so it's important to deliver important information in various ways. For example, you could have "show and tell" meetings where you screen share and discuss things on screen, create visual graphics of steps in a process and verbally reiterate those steps, or share a video that explains recent market developments. Touch base frequently with clients. Especially if you have clients who may be caregiver to elderly or ailing relatives or who are older themselves, make sure that they feel that you are available to answer their questions. Consider sending a weekly or monthly round-up of investment news or other industry updates that could affect their financial plans. Print versions of these are especially helpful for those who may not be tech-savvy.

CHAPTER 5

Innovative Marketing Strategies for Financial Advi

When advertising your services as a financial advisor, a picture of an older couple excitedly enjoying retirement is common. It gets the message across, but it's a bit cliché. In today's market, it pays to think outside of the box and offer creative, specific strategies that cater to marketing financial advice. While online marketing is one of the most important and often cost-effective ways to grab potential clients' attention, there is still a lot of value in traditional marketing options, such as direct mail, social media, and most recently, video. A lot of advisors in our program are having great success with hosting their own educational workshops.

When thinking about giving a seminar, consider the area in which you live and the people who contribute to the community. Giving more specific topics with a local flare could make you stand out in a sea of competition. Some financial advisors take the money they would be paying for online leads and instead invest it into charity events. Discuss with organizations about paid sponsorships that can get your information out to potential clients. Another "outside the box" idea for meeting potential clients is to ask local organizations that are celebrating employee milestones or sales benchmarks if their company would like to have a financial advisor come speak to help motivate employees, discuss what they could be doing in terms of investing in their 401k, and that it would be at no cost to the company. A unique marketing tool is presenting yourself as a grocery store inspection station, titled "Margarita Checkpoint," to inspect the bags for the proper ingredients to benefit charity. Potential leads come to expect this station every year. A more intricate marketing plan is what the creator calls his "MoneyLocker." This black, oversized cooler is filled with a variety of beverages (in room temp), and it's presented closed with a professional sign and photos – sometimes with local celebs – on the top of the cooler. Then he lets his clients and prospects on his VIP lists know about the upcoming office event and even why he thinks everything in cracking in the financial world, but how his "Free SIP-N-TIP" meeting will share invaluable financial insight that you can't get anywhere else. Most of it is done via mailers, brochures, and even brief chats post church. With this marketing strategy, his office actually serves as something of a prophesier for his next seminar. His office is set up as a pro mixer and it differs through a bull pen to an upscale luxurious feel with a set-up drawing from terrace suites. Most of the marketing and lead generation consumes almost one Saturday per month. This financial advisor still sees regular clients during the week. Creating more of a video press kit could make your business stand out, rather than just using a DVD.

The insurance company rep package consists of a variety of marketing strategies, but more often than not these reps don't realize that direct mail and a couple of client dinners a year, though effective, are not the end of a Marketing Plan. We advise having a direct mail campaign with an 18-month marketing calendar, with sequences for appointment setting, events, and more. The retirement planning business is not about money; it's about errand routing, social work, and marketing. Recall that marketing is planned not when you want the doors blowing off from one seminar, but in 18 months when all your marketing efforts have compounded, and now you're slammed with seminars and appointments. Wondering freeing up some time? This is the strategy to accomplish that. You'd have to try pretty hard not to find anyone who needs life or health insurance, or information on how to invest their money better or about IRAs. Every business, every walk of life, is competition. Only within our business there are about 308,749 other licensed agents as of 2016. You have to be good. And sometimes that just isn't enough. Consider yourself, your demographic, and your area. Now, figure out what's going to work for you as a financial advisor.

Digital Marketing Trends

In the ever-changing world of digital marketing, there have been great strides influencing platforms and tactics. This has been seen with updates and integrations in social media, such as Instagram adding a checkout feature, Google adding 3D Shopping, and Facebook expanding stores. New mobile ad formats and strategies have also come to the forefront, with a specific focus on disruptors such as Clubhouse and TikTok. Innovations in search engine marketing and optimization present additional strategies for financial advisors to reach potential clients.

Trends like these are excellent fodder for content. Your job is to take that information and structure it in a way that makes sense for your clients. What's the headline? Use the opportunity of these shifts in trends to create content dripping with best practices for the different platforms or features these disruptors are known for. For example, in Clubhouse's case, you may want to talk about the history of social media platforms, and how from the prominence of photo sharing apps came the rising importance for a 360° omnichannel client experience. This could be tied to separate articles on the different digital platforms, their purpose (professional or personal), and features that really set them apart. The important thing to remember is not to simply relay what you read back to your clients and call it a day. You need to position this content as a unique and valuable resource.

CHAPTER 6

The Importance of Continuing Education and Profess

Given the rapid advancement and development of the economy, it is more important than ever for financial advisors to continue their education and career development. The industry is always changing; therefore, it is indispensable that professionals in the field update and increase their knowledge base constantly. It is critical that a financial advisor attends and applies the latest industry trends and updates from any professional development meetings he or she attends. If there are technological advances, additional programs, legal changes, investment strategies, etc. suggested at the session, be sure to use that information and share it with clients. This is the best way to effectively apply the knowledge gained and, in turn, reap the maximum benefits.

Over time, a financial advisor that consistently shows a concern for career development and increased industry knowledge will see a significant change in his or her advisory practice. Representatives of the National Commission for Certifying Agencies have stated that "ongoing career and professional development for professionals is not only necessary, but it can also lead to further specialization, greater expert advisement, treatment of complex and complicated issues, and higher-quality professional services." VanWie expressed that continuing education and professional development is also a great way to network with colleagues and get new ideas that can take an advisor's service to the next level. Watching a client's financial health soar can be the most rewarding part of a profession in financial consulting.

Industry Certifications and Designations

In late 2009 or so, we decided to explore a career move. I had been a pharmacist for many years and had completed all the education, internships, and certifications and passed the licensure exams to become a registered pharmacist. The requirements are surprisingly similar to what financial advisors go through today, right down to the required "continuing education" credits to keep abreast of changes in the industry.

Like most financial advisors, we were loaded up with industry certifications and designations, both for marketing purposes and because they are essential to knowing what matters most to your clients. Comprehensive financial plans and solutions require a broad and deep understanding of all the things that can impact the lives of our prospects and clients. We did not start with all these designations, however. When we started building our practice in 2011, we had a lot of them, but not all, and we focused on five designations beyond the Certified Financial Planner, or CFP, that we found to be what really mattered to our clients. Even then, we were late to this game. When I started in 2011, 30%+ of new clients selected us over all the other options after seeing our credentials certified that we know how to help them in the areas of their lives that matter to them. Every year major U.S. companies in 13 different industries conducted and published "independent" research into what was most important to their clients. In order, here are the top three things their clients wanted:

Very little has changed in the top three for more than 15 years, but there has been a "brief" shift in some order in what all their clients want fourth. Let me put this in terms of our industry: 65% of our profession positions as the most important value proposition, by far, that they can help protect and grow their clients' wealth over the long term. Only 0.07% of the top advisors across the country position helping clients redefine their future, knowing when they have enough money, and then guiding them toward making it happen as the part of their value proposition that matters most to clients who are expecting to need long-term wealth management advice.

Ethical Considerations in Financial Advisory Pract

Ethical dilemmas in financial advisory practice The specific guidelines for ethical behavior for CFP practitioners, as represented by the CFP Board of Standards and Professional Conduct, apply to both the property and the clients they serve. With regard to the technical nature of the knowledge possessed, CFPs have a fiduciary duty to their clients. Since planners are individuals who possess specialized knowledge, skill, experience, and information not available to the public, this knowledge should be sought by those who need and can benefit from it. Financial planning, at a minimum, is often based on clients' dreams. A fiduciary's role also encompasses helping clients achieve their dreams in ways that make sense given their financial resources, tolerance for risk, the economy, career expectations, and future uncertainties. A conflict of interest in the practice of financial planning is that the power to allocate funds and resources lies uniquely with the planner. Fiduciaries of all types must exercise the utmost care to avoid any conflicts of interest. If all parties do not agree on a conflict, the planner should disclose every financial relationship in advance. Conducting business with a competitor may be ethically permissible as long as it is disclosed in advance. Conducting business with friends, as opposed to strangers, creates a greater degree of trust between all parties involved in a transaction. This is the basis for much of the long-term success in investment and insurance careers. One way to avoid lawsuits is to be patient, faithful, honest, straightforward, serve the public good, do what you say you'll do to the best of your ability, on time, and under close personal supervision. Fees count as well. Investors place a high value on dealing with an advisor who is competent and ethical. Safe harbor for financial advisors means that they will not attract any enforcement attention if they disclose all aspects of their practice. They can also receive compensation as long as the client is aware of it. Firms will not be held liable for endorsing products as long as the person endorsing the product discloses all compensation received. Since advisors should be experts at reducing risk and protecting other people's money and lives, their utmost mission should be to do no harm. However, it is important to note that risk cannot be completely eliminated.

Best Practices for Ethical Decision Making

Here we have a strong alignment between our expectations of what might be in the text and the likelihood of finding a section like this in the textbook. The principle of integrity is a core component expected of financial advisors and organizations overall. To support integrity, individuals need to have strong abilities to make ethical decisions. In having a section such as Best Practices for Ethical Decision-Making, this is where I would expect to find an adaptation of relevant secondary research literature around ethical decision-making and possibly two to three select decision-making processes or frames from that literature, and any added dimensions to the process (as the authors suggest might be appropriate for an ethics-based decision model). The outcome would give an advisor something to draw from when faced with challenges that might call into question their integrity when offering advice—they would have a succession of steps to follow to ensure an ethical resolution.

Given the likely content of this section, the introductory statement that 'Ethical decision-making can be supported by the selection of a best decision-making process and the best practices for using it' is drawn from the summary of what is likely to be included from the following subsection. This next sentence gives an apparent action—a directive using the active voice—that tells readers they can apply the practices to support their ability to make an ethical decision. This subsection about best practices continues to be an overview of the content included in the subheading, indicating a review of decision-making literature and the potential five steps that could provide a complete or enhanced frame for making an ethical decision. The work from which deductions are drawn for this section is cited at the end of the paper.

CHAPTER 8

The Future of Financial Advisory Practice

Subject-matter experts predict that the following are the key trends to watch in 2022-2023, some of which could have a significant impact on financial advisory practice:

1) The ESG movement 2) The rise of mass-affluent households 3) Fiduciary versus suitability standards 4) Remote work 5) A lack of standardization in 'retiring' values 6) External competition

An article at ThinkAdvisor.com reviews several of these trends and is worth a deeper dive. Watching these doesn't have to be a full-time job, but it should form the background of any executive firm's long-term strategic plan, either to capitalize on growth trends or safeguard against industry contractions. The above list of trends is non-exclusive. Certainly, other factors will have an effect on the business in the future. But any potential plans to put into action must take trends such as those listed into account, and any attempts to foresee or model the future should take a holistic view of our environment. In other words, if you are a fee-only or fee-and-commission advisor, your business model must be able to adapt to changes in the marketplace.

Advisory practices that are specialized and offer meaningful value or that are rooted in one or more clearly discernable differentiators have a decent likelihood of being able to engage in something akin to "scarcity pricing" for their services. This does not have to mean they are necessarily charging their clients a premium. Rather, it refers to the idea that the advisors in question can charge a fair price for what they do without necessarily having to go through the usual "song and dance" of charging the lowest price possible.

Trends and Predictions

The future of financial advisory practice will see a shift from a product-centric business to a client-centric one. Developing the right products will not be as important as developing the right way to deliver those products to your clients, keeping in mind that while businesses may have mass, advice is for the individual. A successful advisor will need the tools to be an institution and the products that are designed specifically for them to use as advisors. Your value proposition will be the basis for everything you do. You will need to be constantly aware of what that is, or should be, in order for your clients to want to deal with you when they have many different options. If that vision is not based in advice and the use of product as the delivery tool, you should not be reading the rest of this paper.

In the future, the survivor of the marketplace will be the advisor. The level of importance that you have depends on what kind of an advisor you are. Any advisor can value-add a product, and anyone can make a lot of money on a fee-for-service based on transaction-like business. In the future, those will be the two businesses that have the lowest value.

Your individual experience will be the basis for your success, not your use of a third-party manager. A new world of globalization has started to develop for the end of the majors as we knew them. Any advisor can add value to an investment. If you are nothing but an investment advisor, that is the overused commodity in the next wave. The individual advisor will stand out because they can add value to the investments offered as advice. The individual advice will demand the value offer of knowledge. Any value adder is an escalator that is going to become commonplace in the fee-based, discretionary world. All the things that have a value in this analysis in the future are competencies that the institution should have. We believe that the most successful advisors of the future will be seen as their own institution.